b24-95

Mahogany the Mystery Glider

Mahogany
the Mystery Glider

by Jill Morris

illustrated by Sharon Dye

Greater Glider Productions, Maleny, Queensland, Australia

thanks to
Dr Steve Van Dyck, Bruce Cowell, Greg Czechura, Steve Wilson, Patrick Couper & Chris Burwell, Queensland Museum; Keith Smith, David Flett & Rusty Smith, Queensland Parks & Wildlife Service; Megan Thomas & Dr Gordon Guymer, Queensland Herbarium; Debbie Hotchkis & Greg Thompson, Fleays Wildlife Sanctuary, Burleigh Heads; Virginia McGrath & Wendy Craven, Ingham; Simon Bryant, Scott Burnett & Greg Calvert, Townsville; Jenny Smith, Mission Beach; and Dr Stephen Jackson, Healesville Sanctuary, Victoria.

edited by Dr Steve Van Dyck, Dr Stephen Jackson, Keith Smith & Cheryl Wickes
designed by Lynne Muir
typeset by Range Rose, Maleny QLD
printed by Fergies, Hamilton QLD
(using environmentally friendly waterless printing process)
bound by Podlich, Stafford QLD

illustrated in pencil, gouache and watercolour by Sharon Dye, on paper stained with coffee. Sharon's pictorial reference included materials provided by the Queensland Museum and photographs and samples collected by Jill Morris in the field.

Cataloguing-in-Publication

Morris, Jill, 1936-.
  Mahogany the mystery glider.

  Bibliography.
  Includes index.
  ISBN 0 947304 42 8.

  1. Mahogany glider - Queensland - Juvenile literature. 2. Endangered species - Queensland - Juvenile literature. I. Dye, Sharon. II. Title.

  599.23

© text & pictures Jill Morris & Sharon Dye 1999
© design & format Greater Glider Productions 1999

Thanks to the Australia Council via the Australian Society of Authors for an Illustrator's Grant to Sharon; and to Arts Queensland for financial assistance with travel for Jill's research.

arts
Queensland

Contents

Endangered!	6
Where We Are Found	7
My Family	8
Gliders Take Off!	10
The Mystery of the Skins	12
Changes to Our Habitat – Poem	14
Our Home: Flora	16
Our Home: Fauna	18
Footprints on Flowers – Food	20
Glider in a Gumboot	22
Glider in a Python	23
Hogney and Shoo-Shoo	24
References	30
Glossary	31
Index	32

Endangered!

I am a Mahogany Glider. My scientific name is *Petaurus gracilis*, which means 'slender rope-dancer'. I am a mammal and a marsupial. I am regarded as a mystery because I was 'missing' for 106 years while my species was confused with other gliders. I am endangered because my woodland habitat is continually being destroyed.

Where We Are Found

Mahogany Gliders have been found between Tully and Ingham in a 110 kilometre strip of north Queensland, edged by the Great Barrier Reef and offshore islands. We live close to the coast in lowland forest. Much of our habitat has been cleared for sugar, bananas, pine forests and pineapples, cattle grazing and aquaculture.

My Family

Gliders have been around for about 30 million years.
Six glider species are found in Australia.

Mahogany Gliders belong to the family Petauridae.

We were named after the colour of our fur and the Swamp Mahogany trees in our habitat. We have a very dark stripe reaching from above the nose, over the head and right down the back towards the tail.

Each Mahogany Glider needs a range of at least 20 hectares, with a variety of food trees flowering at different seasons.

The gliding membrane or 'patagium' is dark-coloured with a light edge. We make long gliding swoops (30-60 metres) from tree trunk to tree trunk.

We have very big hands and feet. Each forefoot has five clawed toes and each hindfoot has four clawed toes and one clawless 'thumb'. The second and third toes of the hindfoot are joined together for grooming.

We have large brown eyes and a pointed snout. Our ears are large and hairless.

We are usually born in pairs between April and September. Our life span is about six years.

Our average length is 600mm from the head to the tip of the tail (the body about 250mm and the tail 350mm).

Our home dens are in hollows, often with tiny entrances for safety from predators.

When disturbed or trapped we make URRRGGGAAA sounds.

Gliders Take Off!

With a built-in parachute attached to my wrists, and using my tail as a rudder, I glide from tree to tree like a silent ghost.

l to r: Sugar Glider, Squirrel Glider, Mahogany Glider, Yellow-bellied Glider, Feathertail Glider, Greater Glider (approximately to scale)

With the help of my sharp claws and tail I climb up a steep trunk – then take off! Landing requires a strong grip. Occasionally I miss – and tumble onto the forest floor.

Feathertail is the smallest of the gliders; the Greater Glider is the largest. I am sometimes mistaken for a Sugar Glider but I am twice the length and four times the weight. When I am gliding you can identify me by my long tail.

Nº 12

The Mystery of the Skins

In 1882 a glider skin was sent from 'north of Cardwell' to the director of the Queensland Museum, who described it as a new species *Belideus gracilis*. Without seeing the skin or a live specimen, scientists later decided it must have been a Squirrel Glider. The true identity of the species remained a mystery for more than a hundred years.

In 1974 a glider skin was collected and tagged by Dr Greg Gordon. It came from a woodland near Barrett's Lagoon, south-east of Tully.

In the 1980s the Museum's curator of mammals Steve Van Dyck became curious about three very old glider skins with tags saying they came from 'Mt Echu' (sic). For four years he searched in vain around Mt Echo in north Queensland for live specimens.

In 1989, after the Museum was moved and old collections were being explored, Steve found Dr Gordon's glider in a drum of uncatalogued specimens and noticed its similarity to the 'Mt Echu' skins.

He and Paul Stumkat made a field trip to Barrett's Lagoon. After three nights of searching, their spotlight picked up a glider leaping from a bloodwood tree. They chased it but lost it among the wattles.

They had seen a glider that had been 'missing' for 106 years!

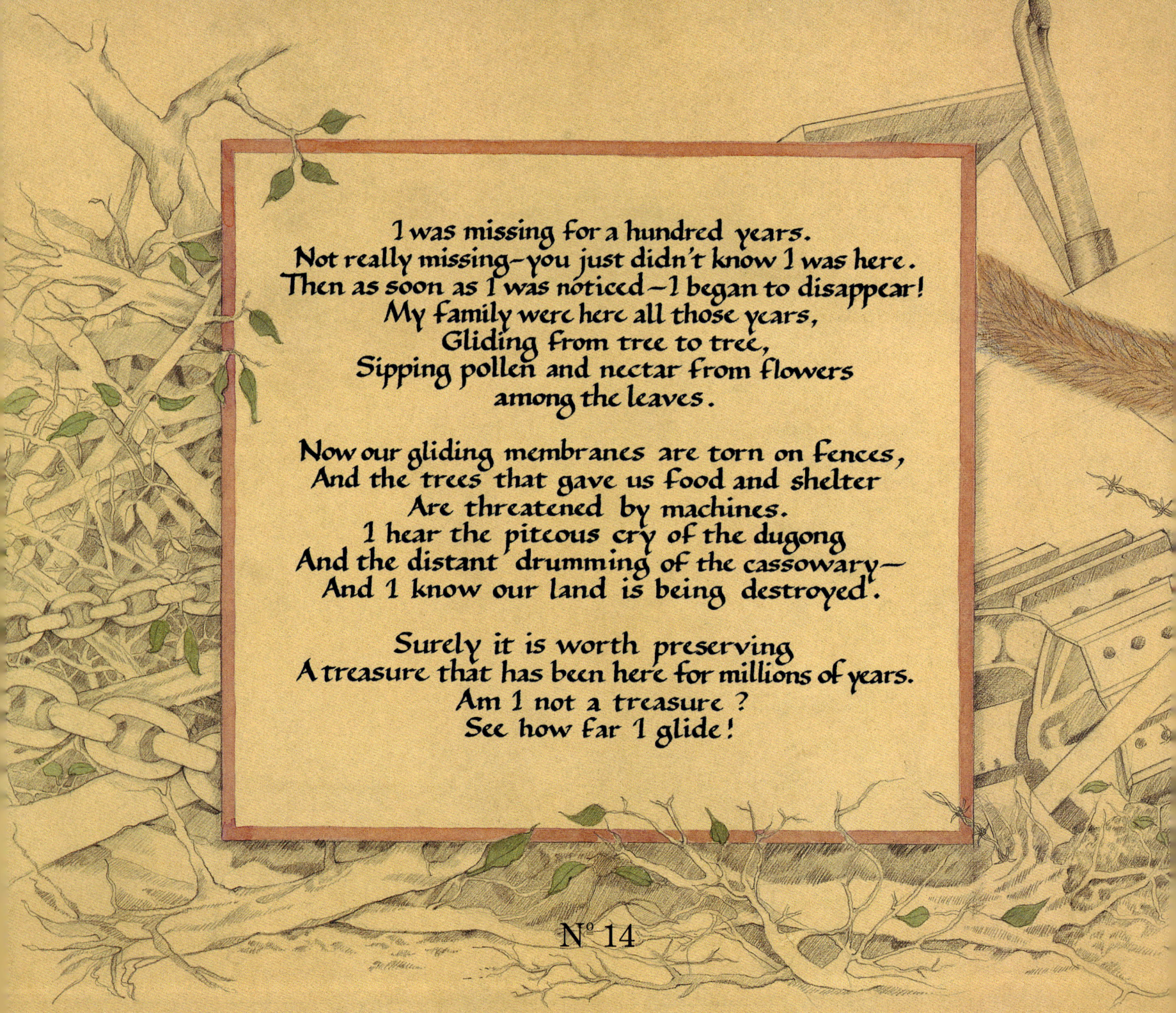

I was missing for a hundred years.
Not really missing—you just didn't know I was here.
Then as soon as I was noticed—I began to disappear!
My family were here all those years,
Gliding from tree to tree,
Sipping pollen and nectar from flowers
among the leaves.

Now our gliding membranes are torn on fences,
And the trees that gave us food and shelter
Are threatened by machines.
I hear the piteous cry of the dugong
And the distant drumming of the cassowary—
And I know our land is being destroyed.

Surely it is worth preserving
A treasure that has been here for millions of years.
Am I not a treasure?
See how far I glide!

Mahogany Glider, Apollo Jewel Butterfly, Masked Owl, Azure Kingfisher, Agile Wallaby, White-lipped Tree Frog, Pale Field-rat

Nº 15

Grass crowds around the feet of tall gums.

Orchids droop from the branches of the trees and waterlilies float on quiet billabongs.

The Ant Plant, growing high on a branch of a melaleuca, makes a home for caterpillars of the Apollo Jewel Butterfly.

Nº 17

Fauna

As we climb at night through the woodland, we watch out for owls, pythons and goannas. Flying-foxes compete with us for flower-food.

l to r: Amethystine Python, Little Red Flying-fox, Sacred Kingfisher, Northern Barred Frog, Rufous Owl, Freshwater Crocodile, Scarlet Honeyeater, Southern Cassowary

While smaller birds sleep, the Rufous Owl and Masked Owl are alert, waiting for us to glide by. Rare northern frogs sing a chorus from the swamp. Crocodiles glide in the deeper billabongs.

At dawn Cassowaries stalk the forest gathering fruits in brilliant colours.

Footprints on Flowers

We scrape the stalks of Grasstrees with our teeth and return later to eat the sticky sap leaking from the gash. We leave our footprints in the white waxy powder on the stalks. We lick the sweet nectar from the tiny white star flowers that shine with moisture in the moonlight.

We scoop scale insects off twigs and leaves of Large-fruited Red Mahogany trees. We sometimes eat Green Tree Ants.

l to r: Grasstree, lichen, Green Tree Ants, scale insects, Beach Wattle & aril, Longicorn grub, Brown Bunyip cicada, purple Christmas Beetle, Apollo Jewel Butterfly, (green) katydid, Pink Bloodwood

Nº 20

We eat the gummy strings (arils) that hold the seeds in the pods of wattle trees.

We lick the leaking sap and blood-red kino from the trunk of bloodwood trees. We eat lichen, moths, beetles, cicadas, grasshoppers, katydids, spiders and ants.

We eat the fruit of mistletoe and many different flowers. The nectar gives us sugar; the pollen gives us protein.

Glider in a Gumboot

When Steve Van Dyck was first trying to catch Mahogany Gliders for radio-tracking, he went out on a casual walk late one night and saw a glider feeding on a Grasstree flower – but he had no net or trap.

He took off one of his gumboots, pushed the glider inside and folded over the top. When he later shook the contents of the boot into a pillowcase – the pillowcase was empty! His prize had hung on to the inside of the boot, and was now balanced on the edge, about to take off. Steve pounced – and caught it.

Later Steve caught other gliders near Barrett's Lagoon by attaching nest boxes made of PVC pipe to tree trunks. One of his captives was called 'Gracie'. Steve took Gracie to Brisbane for a few weeks to study her. She was fed with insects and nectar from flowers. Gracie loved climbing over Steve's head.

'She thought I was a tree!' he said.

Gracie was returned to the wild. The following year Steve found her in the same den tree where she had been caught. With her were young Mahogany Glider twins.

Glider in a Python

In 1996 Stephen Jackson was studying Mahogany Gliders in an area near Cardwell in connection with his PH D thesis at James Cook University.

He had attached radio collars to a number of gliders to enable him to follow their movements. His transmitter picked up a signal from one of the collars – so clearly that he thought the animal had pulled it off and left it on the ground.

Stephen traced the signal to a patch of long grass at the base of a tree. He pulled back the grass and found a three metre 'scrub' python asleep with a lump in its belly and scratches along its side. The glider had put up a good fight.

Every glider trapped by Stephen had been implanted with a microchip for identification. He ran his scanner over the snake. It confirmed that the glider was inside.

On his next trip, Stephen tracked down the missing collar in the python's faeces, along with lots of glider hair.

Over the two years of the study, some children from the local community assisted in trap-monitoring, measuring and release.

Hogney and Shoo-Shoo

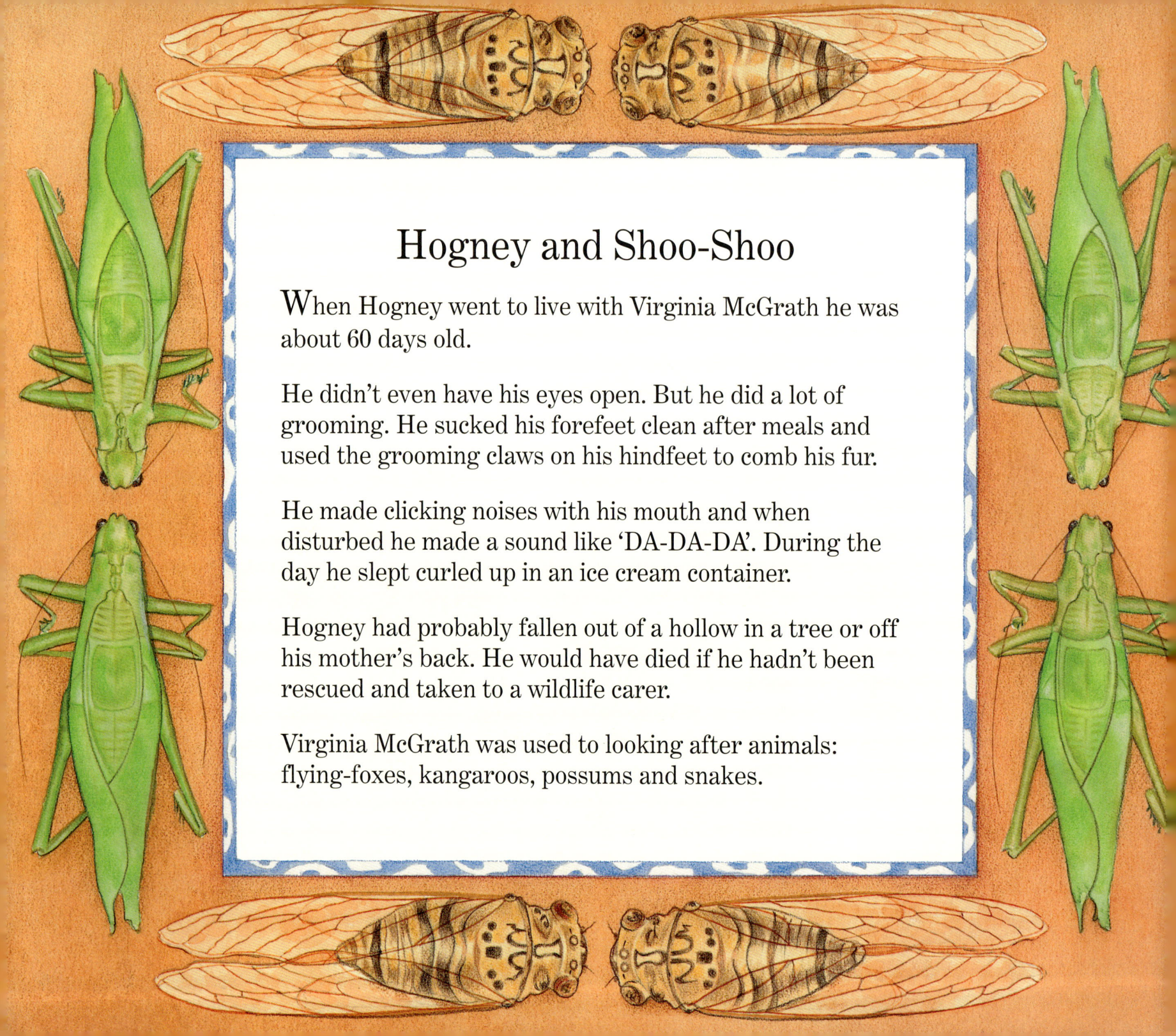

When Hogney went to live with Virginia McGrath he was about 60 days old.

He didn't even have his eyes open. But he did a lot of grooming. He sucked his forefeet clean after meals and used the grooming claws on his hindfeet to comb his fur.

He made clicking noises with his mouth and when disturbed he made a sound like 'DA-DA-DA'. During the day he slept curled up in an ice cream container.

Hogney had probably fallen out of a hollow in a tree or off his mother's back. He would have died if he hadn't been rescued and taken to a wildlife carer.

Virginia McGrath was used to looking after animals: flying-foxes, kangaroos, possums and snakes.

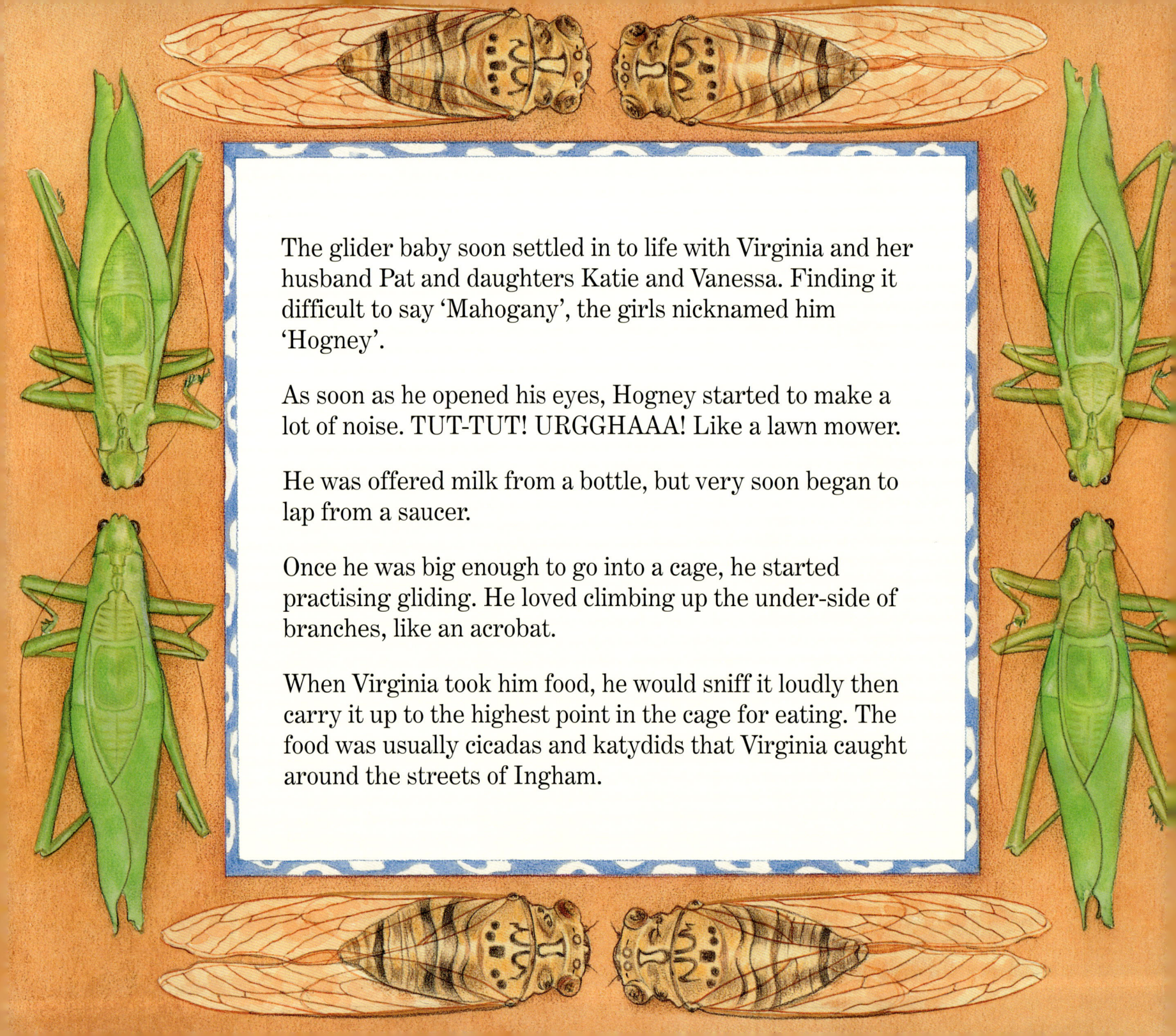

The glider baby soon settled in to life with Virginia and her husband Pat and daughters Katie and Vanessa. Finding it difficult to say 'Mahogany', the girls nicknamed him 'Hogney'.

As soon as he opened his eyes, Hogney started to make a lot of noise. TUT-TUT! URGGHAAA! Like a lawn mower.

He was offered milk from a bottle, but very soon began to lap from a saucer.

Once he was big enough to go into a cage, he started practising gliding. He loved climbing up the under-side of branches, like an acrobat.

When Virginia took him food, he would sniff it loudly then carry it up to the highest point in the cage for eating. The food was usually cicadas and katydids that Virginia caught around the streets of Ingham.

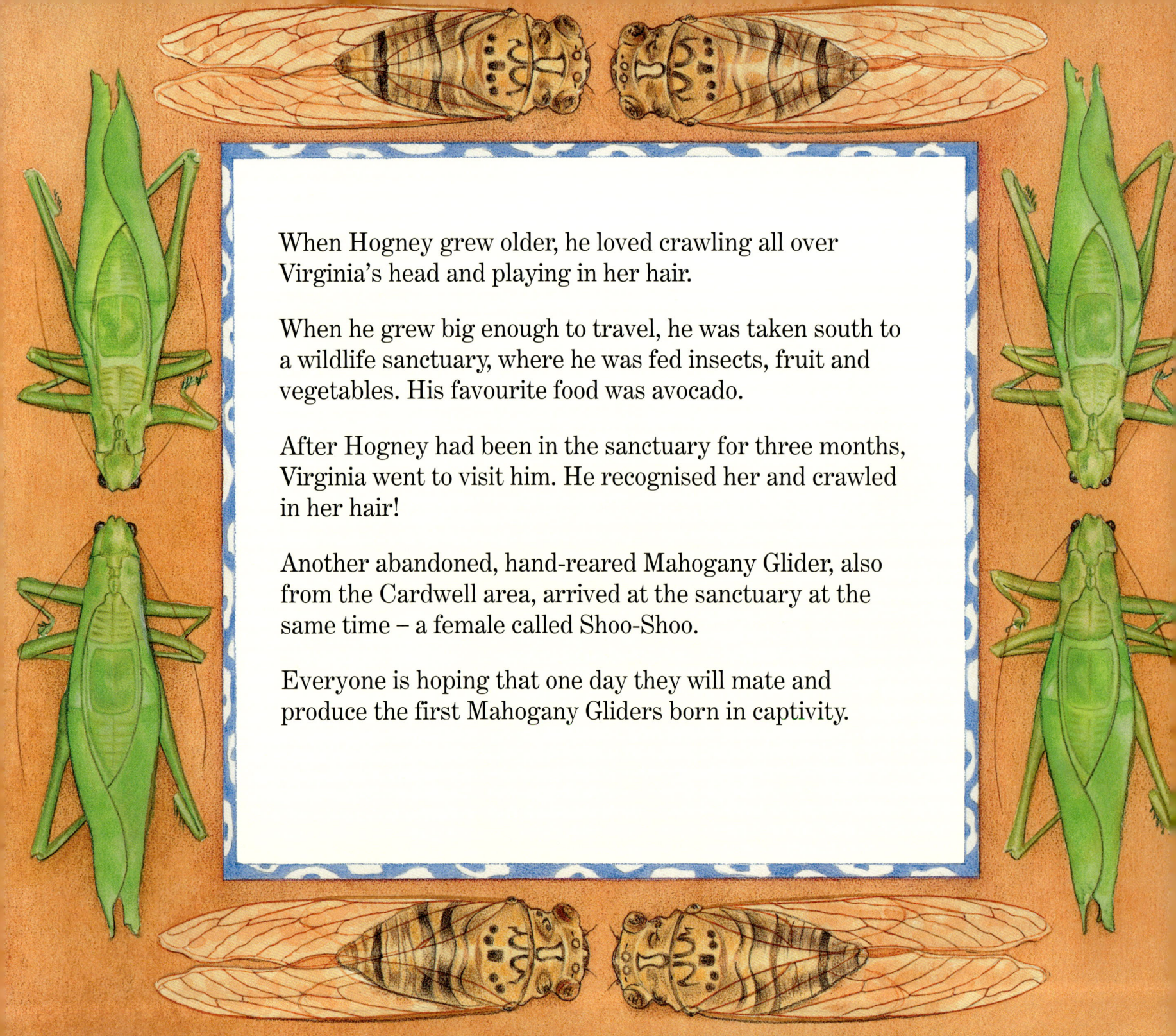

When Hogney grew older, he loved crawling all over Virginia's head and playing in her hair.

When he grew big enough to travel, he was taken south to a wildlife sanctuary, where he was fed insects, fruit and vegetables. His favourite food was avocado.

After Hogney had been in the sanctuary for three months, Virginia went to visit him. He recognised her and crawled in her hair!

Another abandoned, hand-reared Mahogany Glider, also from the Cardwell area, arrived at the sanctuary at the same time – a female called Shoo-Shoo.

Everyone is hoping that one day they will mate and produce the first Mahogany Gliders born in captivity.

References

Cotsell, N. & Jackson, S. 1996. *Sweet Success for the Mahogany Glider.* Nature Australia Magazine, Winter.

Flannery, T. illus Schouten, P. 1994. *Possums of the World - A Monograph of the Phalangeroidea.* Geo Productions, Sydney.

Jackson, S. 1997. *Mahogany Gliders.* Australian Geographic Volume 47, Sydney, July-Sept.

Jackson, S. & Johnson, C. 1998. *Behavioural Ecology of the Mahogany Glider Petaurus gracilis (Petauridae: Marsupialia).* Final report prepared for the Queensland Department of Environment (unpublished).

Strahan, R. 1995. *Mammals of Australia.* Australia Museum/Reed Books, Sydney.

Van Dyck, S. 1991. *Raising an old glider's ghost.* Wildlife Australia Magazine, Winter.

Van Dyck, S. 1992. *Lasting Impressions of Mahogany Gliders.* Nature Australia Magazine, Spring.

Van Dyck, S. 1993. *The Taxonomy and Distribution of Petaurus gracilis (Marsupialia: Petauridae), with Notes on its Ecology and Conservation Status.* Memoirs of the Queensland Museum, Brisbane.

Dr Steve Van Dyck

Glossary

acacia – wattle tree
Acrobates – (scientific) acrobat
aquaculture – land-based farming of water life
aril – the gummy string that holds wattleseeds in a pod
australis – (scientific) southern
breviceps – (scientific) short head
digit – finger
faeces – excrement, droppings
gracilis – slender
implanted – inserted into the skin
katydid – a type of grasshopper with long feelers
kino – the gum that leaks from a tree wound
lichen – like moss, growing on a tree
mammal – animal that suckles its young
marsupial – animal that looks after young in a pouch
microchip – small chip for storing electronic data
melaleuca – paperbark/tea-tree
nectar – sweet substance produced by flowers
patagium – a fold of skin extending from the body in gliding mammals and reptiles
Petaurus – (scientific) tightrope-walker; rope-dancer
phyllodes – 'leaves' with no central vein
pollen – fine dust produced by flowers
pygmaeus – pygmy
sap – the juice of plants
sic – written that way
volans – (scientific) flying

Dr Stephen Jackson

Index

acacias (wattles) 16-17,20-21
Acacia mangium 16-17
Agile Wallaby *Macropus agilis* 15
Amethystine Python *Morelia amethistina* 18
Ant Plant *Myrmecodia beccarii* 17
Apollo Jewel Butterfly *Hypochrysops apollo apollo* 15,16-17,20-21
arils 21
Azure Kingfisher *Alcedo asurea* 15
Barbed Wire Vine *Smilax* 16
Barretts Lagoon 13,22
Beach Wattle *Acacia crassicarpa* 20-21
Belideus gracilis 13
billabongs 17,19
Blady Grass 16-17
Blue Tongue *Melastoma affine* 16
Cairns 7
Cardwell 7,13,23,28
Cassowary, Southern *Casuarius casuarius* 14,18-19
cicadas 21,24,26,28
Dugong *Dugong dugon* 14
eucalypts 16
Feathertail Glider *Acrobates pygmaeus* 10-11
Flying-foxes 18,24
Freshwater Crocodile *Crocodylus johnstoni* 18-19
goannas 9,18
Gordon, Dr Greg 13
Grasstree, *Xanthorrhoea johnsonii* 20,22
Great Barrier Reef 7
Greater Glider *Petauroides volans* 10-11
Green Tree Ant *Oecophylla smaragdina* 16,20
Ingham 7,26
Innisfail 7
Jackson, Dr Stephen 23,31
James Cook University 23
katydids 20-21,24,26,28
kino 21
Large-fruited Red Mahogany *Eucalyptus pellita* 16,20
lichen 20-21
Little Red Flying-fox *Pteropus scapulatus* 18
Masked Owl *Tyto novaehollandiae* 15,19
McGrath, Virginia & family 24,26,28
melaleucas 16-17
mistletoe 21
Mt Echu 13
Mt Echo 13
Northern Barred Frog *Mixophyes schevilli* 18
orchids 16-17
Pale Field-rat *Rattus tunneyi* 15
patagium 8
phyllodes 16-17
Pink Bloodwood *Corymbia intermedia* 20-21
pythons 18,23
Queensland 7,13
Queensland Museum cover,13
Rufous Owl *Ninox rufa* 18-19
Sacred Kingfisher *Todiramphus sanctus* 18
Scarlet Honeyeater *Myzomela sanguinolenta* 18-19
Squirrel Glider *Petaurus norfolcensis* 10,13
Stumkat, Paul 13
Sugar Glider *Petaurus breviceps* 10-11
Swamp Mahogany 8
Townsville 7
Tully 7,13
Van Dyck, Dr Steve cover,13,22,30
waterlilies 16-17
White-lipped Tree Frog *Litoria infrafrenata* 15
Yellow-bellied Glider *Petaurus australis* 10-11